REBOUND
rituals

Rebound Rituals

5O Ways to Bounce Back After Breaking Up

BY *Kerry Colburn* and *Jennifer Worick*
ILLUSTRATIONS BY *Neryl Walker*

CHRONICLE BOOKS
SAN FRANCISCO

Library of Congress Cataloging-in-Publication Data available.

ISBN 0-8118-4546-X

Manufactured in China.

Designed by Laura Crookston

Distributed in Canada by Raincoast Books
9050 Shaughnessy Street
Vancouver, British Columbia V6P 6E5

10 9 8 7 6 5 4 3 2 1

Chronicle Books LLC
85 Second Street
San Francisco, California 94105
www.chroniclebooks.com

DISCLAIMER: THE AUTHORS ARE
NOT RESPONSIBLE FOR ANY PAIN,
PHYSICAL OR OTHERWISE, INFLICTED
ON AN UNDESERVING, UNREPENTANT,
UNSAVORY EX. BOYS, WATCH YOUR BACKS.

This book is dedicated to anyone who has weathered a broken heart—may your recovery be swift and your new life glorious!

We've all been through tough times. Love hasn't always been kind. Subpar partners haven't always lived up to their promises. And your friends' well-meaning sentiments like "You'll get through it," "You're better off without him," and "Living well is the best revenge" don't always ease the pain.

There's no way around it:

breakups suck, no matter what. The thing is, it's okay to be really pissed off and scream about how you were wronged. (You were!) It's also okay to get weepy and sentimental, even if you know he was unworthy of your sweet self. Mood swings are to be expected and, we say, encouraged. Only by going through the gamut of emotions will you be able to work through the pain and get to a better place, where you're excited by the prospect of kissing someone new or having a crush or making eyes at a stranger across a room.

What you need to sail through the difficult post-breakup stage is activity, fun, friendship, self-love, and a nice healthy dose of extreme self-care. (It also doesn't hurt to reflect frequently on your ex's infinite shortcomings, not the least of which was his less-than-stellar treatment of you!) We understand that you may be irrational, annoyed, depressed, or manic right now. We accept that denial, anger, bargaining, depression, and acceptance—all stages of grief—will surface to some degree after a nasty breakup. But we want you to remember that you are a fantastic, vibrant creature full of possibility, and we want you to realize this as soon as possible. So we've put together a slew of ways for you to feel better *fast*, with something for every mood, time, and energy level. Just flip this book open when you need a lift and pick whatever idea strikes your fancy.

Put simply, *Rebound Rituals* is a way to be really nice to yourself and, at times, be really mean to your ex. (We promise you won't get into any legal trouble with our humorous take on space cleansings, burning ceremonies, voodoo dolls, and poison pen letters!) We suggest many activities to pamper yourself, celebrate your fabulous attributes, and make you ready to face the world again. We think you should try them all. From the simple act of buying new bedding or lingerie to a more involved production of making a home movie chronicling your tortuous breakup, it's time to spoil (and humor) yourself while you rediscover just how sexy and desirable you are.

So indulge. Relax. Explore. Drink. Cry. Sing. Wallow if you need to. For once, it's all about *you,* and you deserve it all. Be as selfish and self-absorbed as you want to be . . . and then get out there and show the world what you've got. There's something (and someone) new and unexpected waiting for you, right around the corner.

Get ready to rebound!

—Kerry and Jennifer

fly solo

Have you always wanted to see New Orleans? Would you love to take a cooking class in Tuscany, or be pampered at an upscale spa? Did you go to the Rose Bowl with your ex when you really wanted to see the Great Barrier Reef? Now is the time to take a trip that's all about *you*. Celebrate your single status by going exactly where you want to go, and traveling at your own pace. You'll relish your freedom, meet interesting people along the way, and remind yourself that you can do anything you want to do—all by yourself.

If a major vacation isn't in the cards right now, check the Web for low, low fares and take off for a long weekend. Whether it's Montreal for $209 or Miami for $89, pick your destination, throw a red bra and a pair of Jackie O. sunglasses in a tote, and fly solo. Do it now!

name that ex!

Sometimes there's nothing like a little name-calling to elevate your spirits. Try this: From now on, anytime your ex comes up in conversation—or anytime you feel like screaming at him in the privacy of your own apartment—don't use his real name. Don't even call him "my ex." He doesn't deserve to be linked to you. Instead, pick a suitable derogatory nickname and refer to him by it exclusively, whether chatting at a party or writing in your journal. Some (printable) examples to get you started:

worm

DEAD**WEIGHT**

FOOL
Dumbass

POND SCUM *Heel*

RAT Bastard *Jerkwad*

IDIOT *Loser*

HE WHO SHALL NOT BE NAMED

Freak of Nature

momma's boy

BUTTHEAD *DRAG* on the Ticket

PERV Spineless Dolt

*Slime*BALL **THE UNWORTHY**

TAKING HIS NAME AND TURNING IT INTO A TAUNTING,
SCHOOLYARD-STYLE NICKNAME WORKS, TOO.

the art of the hate letter

THE TASTEFUL SMACKDOWN

Letter writing may seem like a boring Jane Austen activity, so liven things up by crafting a missive that strikes the perfect balance between malice and propriety. To wit:

> Dearest Cretin,
>
> It has recently come to my attention that you have been making advances toward my impressionable younger sister, despite her utter lack of interest. I must insist that you stop this perversion immediately. Should you fail to do so, I will have no choice but to take extreme measures to keep you from soiling my gene pool. Let me be plain: by "extreme," I mean pain, suffering, abject misery. Underestimate neither my will nor my malicious imagination.

You get the idea. Even though you won't likely send the letter, make sure it is written in impeccable script on heavy stationery. Signing it in blood might be a little over the top, but red ink—that's an idea!

THE PURGE

If you aren't in touch with your inner Victorian heroine, no sweat. Just cuss like a sailor and write down every mean and nasty thought you have about the rat bastard. Don't hold back—let it rip in one continuous hate frenzy. Spit on your letter for added emphasis, then tear it up. Feel better?

THE "IT'S NOT ME, IT'S YOU" LETTER

Use this handy template as your guide:

Ungrateful (GHASTLY NOUN),

I truly can't believe I spent ____ days/weeks/ months/years of my life on you. You are appallingly (UNPLEASANT ADJECTIVE) and I hate the way you (DISGUSTING HABIT) in front of me. I wish you nothing but (HORRIBLE FATE) and (EMBARRASSING PHYSICAL AILMENT). I'm having so much more (FUN ACTIVITY) and (SEXUAL ACTIVITY) since you've been gone! This is because I've finally realized—it's not me, it's you. Clearly, I deserve a much better partner, like (NAME OF HOTTIE). In fact, I'm already dating him! Your (IRRESISTIBLE ADJECTIVE) ex,

(YOUR NAME)

tarot therapy

It's all in the cards. Find out who and what is in your future by doing a very simple tarot card reading on yourself. Go to your local metaphysical or New Age shop and browse around until you find a set of cards whose color palette or design speaks to you. (Often these shops can refer you to a professional reader, if you want one.) Shuffle the cards, twist some of them end to end, shuffle again, then put them in three stacks, representing past, present, and future. Choose a card from within each stack, place it face up, and see what is revealed. You can also check out the miserable fate awaiting your ex (remember to reshuffle). Tarot decks usually come with a booklet explaining the significance of each card.

the good news is
The WB is verboten no more.

FEEL BETTER FAST: *Practice flirting demurely with every man you encounter, until it comes naturally — make eyes at the bartender, the doorman, and yes, the cute guy at work.*

take time to tango

How many times did you ask your ex to take you dancing—and did he *ever* deliver? If watching *Strictly Ballroom* or *Dirty Dancing* makes you shimmy involuntarily, it's time to sign up for dance lessons. Learn classic ballroom, salsa, swing, hip-hop, or the lambada—it doesn't matter. Taking classes solo guarantees you'll meet new people, including men who have rhythm!

prepare for close encounters of the "ex" kind

It pays to be prepared for the inevitable—running into *him*, especially when you least expect or want it. Here are a few bon mots to have on hand, so you're cool and collected no matter what the circumstances.

the good news is
You can wear granny
panties all the time!

IF YOU RUN INTO HIM . . .

At the gym: "Since we broke up, my workouts have gone to another level. I've even qualified for the Boston Marathon!"

With no makeup: "I'm modeling for a sculptor who prefers to see my perfect bone structure au naturel."

With a doughnut stuffed in your mouth: "Wow, I always need sugar after sex!"

While drunk: "I'm celebrating the huge promotion I got today! Can I buy you a drink? You look like you've had a rough day."

With another girl: "Oh, is this your mom?"

With a group of guys: "I'm so glad your friends have accepted your alternative lifestyle! You told them, right?"

In sweats: "These are way too big for me. Bob's so tall!"

In line at the grocery store: "I'm loading up because we're having Javier's parents over for dinner!"

At a bookstore on a Friday night: "I wanted to pick up a few books for my trip to Paris next week."

Looking fabulous: "Do I know you? Have we met?"

strip it good

A sexy striptease no longer has to be just for his viewing pleasure. Practicing a few moves is a great way to turn yourself on and get in, um, *touch* with your inner vixen—not to mention put you in fine form for your next fling or new and improved boyfriend. Rent a few movies to put you in the mood. While *Striptease* is a horrid movie, Demi does shake it pretty darn well. Jamie Lee Curtis rocks the bedpost in *True Lies*, Kim Basinger turns up the heat in *9½ Weeks*, and Pamela Anderson gyrates as an animated stripper/superhero in Spike TV's *Stripperella*.

When you're fully inspired, turn on some music that moves you and maybe even pick a persona, such as naughty librarian or nurse. Layer your costume over your sauciest lingerie and get busy: Position yourself in front of a mirror and use a chair, bedpost, and any other props around the house to support yourself while slinking, bending, bumping, and grinding. Take your sweet time removing your clothing and building anticipation. And don't forget to slip a few dollar bills in your own G-string. You work hard for the money!

roast the beast

Host a dinner party in your ex's "honor." Invite your pals over for a feast (be sure to include dishes that your former love couldn't stomach or was allergic to). Kick it off with a celebratory Champagne "roast" toast: Ask each guest to come up with one telling anecdote or story that drives home the point that your former hero is a big fat zero. By the end of the evening, surrounded by empty bottles of wine and friends who love you, remind yourself that living well is the best revenge.

create a
dream-life journal

Visualizing what you want is the first step to getting it, and not just in the romance department. A breakup can be the perfect time to reevaluate all aspects of your life: home environment, family relationships, job, circle of friends, wardrobe. Buy a pretty journal and begin writing lists to clarify your short- and long-term desires. What does your ideal home look like? Sketch it out. What are the key characteristics of your dream man? Describe him to a T. Be as specific as you can, and return to your lists at least once a week to refresh your memory and make adjustments. You'll learn a lot about yourself and be on your way to conjuring your dreams into reality.

host a pity party

Gather every single gal you know for a raucous night of bitter dishing and female bonding. Light some candles, arm your guests with drinks (have refills within easy reach) and tasty finger food, sit in a circle, and let it rip. Encourage (or goad) each guest to share both the petty and the grievous offenses that men have committed against her. Inattention, insults, chronic tardiness, cheating, bad kissing technique, Oedipal complexes, addiction to golf, work, or *American Idol*—nothing is too minor to mention, nothing is off limits. End on a positive note by going around the circle and revealing what quality you'd each like to find in your next guy and sharing a tip on where to meet available men.

FEEL BETTER FAST: *Bury the tacky heart-shaped pendant or other bauble he gave you. Plant a thorny rosebush over it and let your pain blossom into beauty.*

assemble an album of worthy males

Before you start thinking all men are unworthy, create a visual reminder of the men you know who redeem their sex. Include brothers, fathers, nice ex-boyfriends, gay friends, co-workers, the Dalai Lama, movie star crushes, and so on. You can also list their best traits as a reminder of what to look for in your future boyfriend(s). Put their photos in either a small, flip-book-style album or on your computer in an electronic album. You might also want to get together with your favorite gal pals to create similar inspiration albums for each of you.

smudge him out

Native Americans understand the power of smudging, the time-honored practice of using sage smoke to cleanse, clarify, and shoo away foul spirits. Create your own Rebound Rod by tying twine (dental floss and shoelaces work in a pinch) around stalks of dried sage, or buy a premade sage stick at an herbal or New Age store. Now, light it and walk throughout your pad, making sure the therapeutic smoke hits areas where his energy might be lingering most (the bed, the remote, the toilet), as well as all corners of every room. Think pure thoughts for the future while it burns. Open all your windows wide to clear the smoke and let in fresh air.

burn,
baby, burn

Collect the last reminders of *him* around the house, such as handwritten notes or photos. (Just be sure to chuck that flame-retardant shirt and his cheesy CDs—breathing toxic fumes isn't very cathartic.) In a safe place, like a fireplace or outdoor grill, light up the burnable items and watch his crap go up in smoke. As you gaze at the flames licking his stack of *Maxim* magazines, visualize any remaining feelings you may have for him—both good and bad—also going up in smoke. Do a little dance. When you've reduced it all to ashes, put out the fire, breathe deeply, and move on, a little bit lighter in both belongings and spirit.

the good news is
**You can have girls' night
any night you want.**

become a gourmet

If you aren't a born chef, consider taking a class to brush up on your culinary talents. And set aside any low-fat recipes or cookbooks. It's time to indulge. Whip up a gourmet meal for yourself and don't forget to pair it with a fabulous wine. Why sob into a bowl of Kraft Mac & Cheese and a Diet Coke when you can be sobbing into a pan of homemade lasagna and a fat glass of Zinfandel?

We're including both a savory and a sweet recipe to set you on the path to culinary bliss. Take comfort in some comfort food, specifically, Jennifer's Lasagna and her Cowgirl Cookies.

JENNIFER'S LASAGNA This is my mother's lasagna recipe and it is a good way to ease any pain. If you want a vegetarian option, simply fold a drained box of frozen chopped spinach into the cheese mixture and forgo the sausage in the sauce. The lasagna can be prepared ahead of time and frozen or refrigerated before cooking. I always keep a tray in the freezer in the event of an emergency (e.g., a nasty breakup).

1 pound spicy Italian sausage
1 onion, chopped
2 cloves garlic, minced or pressed
One 26-ounce jar plus one 14-ounce jar spaghetti sauce
2 cups shredded mozzarella cheese
16 ounces cottage cheese
¼ cup milk
8 ounces (½ box) dried lasagna noodles

Preheat oven to 350°F. Brown the sausage (remove from casings, if necessary) with the onion and garlic in a skillet. Drain grease and then transfer the sausage mixture to a large saucepan. Add the spaghetti sauce and simmer gently. In a bowl, mix together 1¾ cups of the mozzarella, the cottage cheese, and the milk. Set aside ¼ cup of mozzarella to sprinkle on top of the lasagna.

In a 9-by-13-inch lasagna or cake pan, layer your lasagna: First, spread 1¼ cups of sauce on the bottom, then a layer of uncooked noodles, another 1¼ cups of sauce, 2 cups of the cheese mixture, a second layer of noodles, the remaining 1½ cups sauce, and 2 cups cheese mixture. Sprinkle the reserved ¼ cup of mozzarella on top.

Cover with foil. Bake for 30 minutes. Remove foil and bake for an additional 30 minutes or until the cheese on top has browned.

SERVES 6 TO 8
(or one really hungry post-breakup gal and her best friend)

COWGIRL COOKIES These cookies are the perfect sweet to shovel into your mouth when nursing a broken heart. Make sure to have some ice-cold milk on hand for frequent dunking.

- 2 sticks (1 cup) margarine, softened
- 1 cup white sugar
- 1 cup brown sugar
- 2 eggs
- 1 teaspoon vanilla extract
- 2 cups flour
- 1 teaspoon baking soda
- ½ teaspoon baking powder
- 2 cups oatmeal
- 1 package semisweet chocolate chips

Preheat oven to 350°F. In a large bowl, beat together the margarine, white sugar, brown sugar, eggs, and vanilla. In a small bowl, sift together the flour, baking soda, and baking powder, then add to the margarine mixture. Fold in the oatmeal and chocolate chips. Grease and flour a cookie sheet. Place Ping-Pong-size balls of dough about 2 inches apart and bake for 8 minutes. Since oven temperatures vary, keep a close eye on your first batch. At the first hint of browning, take them out. They should be very soft and doughy. Carefully remove cookies with a spatula and allow to cool on a wire rack. Store cookies in an airtight container to keep them soft.

MAKES ABOUT 50 TO 60 COOKIES

the good news is
You know the leftovers
will be in the fridge
in the morning.

FEEL BETTER FAST: *Host a wine tasting at your place—ask everyone to bring a new wine and a new guy that they haven't tried.*

reclaim your bed

Get rid of the bad chi that might be hovering around
your bed. First, clear out everything from under the
bed—it can cause energy to stagnate. Pick out new
bedding, velvet throw pillows, a new mattress if necessary. Revel in an exotic color, a girlie floral pattern,
or whatever style speaks to you and you alone. Buy
that down comforter or chenille duvet cover you've
been eyeballing. Pull out your grandmother's quilt.
Create a bed that will provide maximum solace and
comfort. After washing your new sheets, lightly sprinkle
them with a fragrant dusting powder or spritz them
with sheet spray (lavender promotes good sleep). Climb
in and dream about the men you have yet to meet.

the good news is
Finally, stuffed animals can
come out of storage.

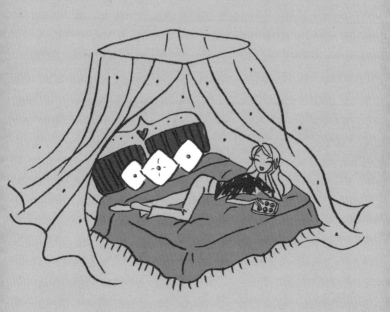

concoct a
signature cocktail

Every sassy single gal should have "her drink." Do
you know what yours is? If not, belly up to a bar with
your best girlfriends and start ordering drinks with
cool names until you find a fave. May we suggest the
French 75 (named for a vintage gun, it's a powerful
choice), the Manhattan (so urbane!), or the Daiquiri
(a real Havana-style one, not an alcoholic slurpee).
Now, perfect it at home. You will find yourself in
demand at parties and will always know what to serve
at your own soirees. Just smile when people gush,
"You make the best Cosmopolitans!" Alternatively,
invent your own drink, using favorite spirits, mixers,
and garnishes. Name it after one of your favorite
body parts or winning qualities (the Saucy Smirk or
the Strut, perhaps?).

Here's a drink to try in warm-weather months, whether with friends on your back porch or out at a bar. Drink two and dream of dashing Italian suitors.

BELLINI

1 ripe peach, peeled and pitted
  Simple syrup (2 parts water, 1 part sugar, heated slowly on stove until sugar dissolves), to taste
5 ounces Prosecco (or other sparkling wine)

Puree the peach and stir in the simple syrup. Spoon 1½ ounces of the peach mixture into a chilled flute and top with the sparkling wine. **Bellissimo!**

SERVES 1 (Repeat as necessary)

dating prep

One of the best things about a breakup is the realization that brand-new men and exciting first dates are in store for you. Revel in your newly single lifestyle by doing some prep work, whether or not you're emotionally ready right now to get back out there. When that day comes, you'll be prepared!

UNMENTIONABLES Devote an entire afternoon to lingerie. Check out small boutiques and good department stores. Try on everything, especially new colors, styles, and cuts. (Don't leave without three matching sets, the boudoir staple of the on-the-market gal.)

SPAS AND SALONS Get those highlights or that cut he was against, try a spray tan, and wax anything that's a bit unruly. Don't let yourself go—looking great will keep your spirits high and besides, you never know when an interesting new man will turn up. Keep your body smooth and supple with massages, mud baths, herbal wraps, or other treatments.

VISUAL MERCHANDISING What are your best assets? Buy one perfect date outfit–with shoes and accessories, of course–that highlights them beautifully.

STAYING CURRENT Read your local papers to find out about hot spots, exhibits, and new restaurants– then try out one a week.

flirting 101

Don't let your flirting skills lie fallow! Follow these simple steps and you'll have new men eating out of your hand. (They're really not that complicated.)

the good news is
There's a whole wide world of men out there!

✴ *Make eye contact, holding his gaze just a second longer than feels comfortable.*

✴ *Use body language: lean in as he's speaking, and lightly touch his arm or shoulder to show warmth and interest.*

✴ *Don't forget how fascinating you are! Have a handful of anecdotes at the ready, whether it's about a recent hike, a wild night out, or a funny trick you taught your dog.*

✴ *Encourage him to open up by asking questions and paying attention.*

✴ *Lick your lips, slowly, while looking at him. (Oldest trick in the book.)*

✴ *If you're feeling brave, toy idly with your spaghetti strap or the top button of your shirt. (Second oldest trick in the book, and as effective as the first.)*

✴ *Don't forget to smile!*

FEEL BETTER FAST: *Get a hot stone foot massage, pedicure with a sizzling shade of nail polish, and some strappy sandals to show off your adorable toes.*

throw a pampering party

Invite a few fabulous females over and dive into a smorgasbord of spa treats, comfort food, and light-hearted chick flicks. Give them mani/pedis, smooth on face masks, and update their makeup with your sauciest new lipstick or sparkly eyeshadow. Be sure to have necessary spa supplies on hand, including fluffy towels, lotion, cotton balls, and headbands, as well as specific materials for various treatments. Along with your spa snacks, serve cranberry juice spritzers or organic green tea to promote a healthy glow. Polishing their outsides will spruce up *your* insides.

harness your chi

Your body's fourth chakra, or energy center, is known as the heart chakra. Located at the heart center, it represents compassion and devotion; in Eastern wisdom, a balanced heart chakra is necessary to give and receive love. Needless to say, after a bad breakup, your heart chakra might be seriously out of whack. We can't have that! Get that positive chi flowing by surrounding yourself with things that encourage a balanced heart chakra: green vegetables; marjoram, neroli, and rose essential oils (try dabbing one on a cotton ball and putting it in your pillowcase); and emerald, rose quartz, and ruby gemstones. (Could it be the perfect excuse to buy that emerald pendant you've had your eye on?) Activities that maintain a balanced heart chakra include volunteering, reading inspirational books, reading or writing poetry, and watching mushy movies. Or try sitting in a comfortable meditation position and repeat "I trust my heart" for three minutes, visualizing the healing emerald-green light of your heart center. This technique releases emotional wounds and calms the mind.

FEEL BETTER FAST: *Call in sick (you are heartsick, after all) and have a day of complete indulgence. Take a bath, watch the soaps, eat ice cream at 10 A.M., catch a matinee . . . in other words, play hooky.*

do unto others

Dump, um, *donate* gifts he gave you to a worthy cause. Give clothes he bought you or really liked on you (that you always thought made you look skanky or like a bag of potatoes) to the Salvation Army. Use the time he used to take up in a positive way by volunteering. Counteract his negative energy with your beneficent soul!

cruise the internet

If you aren't ready to reenter the singles scene, block out a couple evenings a week to take yourself out on the cyber-town. Fix yourself a cocktail, swipe on your sassiest red lipstick, spritz on a sultry fragrance, and slip into your slinkiest lingerie or dress. Now get ready to make eyes at dozens of men! Check out various dating Web sites, set up a profile, and start sending out saucy e-mails to anyone you like the look of. In cyberspace, you can choose a guy just by looks, income, or dog without apology! Simply outline your ideal man and watch the delicious options unfold before you. And best of all, you can wear your highest, fanciest stilettos—since you're not going anywhere, your feet won't hurt!

embrace your space

Now that your single life is starting anew, it's time to make sure everything in your pad is arranged so that you receive maximum benefits, whether it's a sudden monetary windfall or meeting a hot guy. Let the ancient art of feng shui show you the way. Get rid of clutter (especially things that remind you of Jerkwad); toss anything that's cracked, chipped, or broken (you're well on your way after dumping the dead weight); give your entryway some TLC by oiling the hinges, getting a new welcome mat, or painting the door (it mirrors the entrance to your heart); and make sure everything in your space is something you love (especially yourself, sister!).

how to test-drive new men

You shop around a long time for a new car. Why lower your standards for a man? The next time you're evaluating a would-be boyfriend, ponder these questions: How many miles does he seem to have on him? Have there been any unreported relationship crashes? Does he brake on command? Does he come with added features that will make you more comfortable? Does he come prepared for your safety? Will he provide a smooth, luxurious ride? How much insurance will you need? How much will he cost you?

a daily dose of praise

Not getting enough props lately? For a visual pat on the back, create customized cards of your most stellar moments. On a stack of index cards, paste photos of when you felt beautiful and write down the many ways you are uniquely fabulous. Use that photo from your cousin's wedding where you looked like a movie star. Recall the saintly moment when you helped an elderly neighbor. Draw one card every day to remind yourself that you are 32 flavors and then some.

let's talk about sex, baby

Just because you're temporarily flying solo, doesn't mean you have to put your sex life on hold. *Au contraire!* Keep those pheromones in tip-top condition by reading great erotica, such as literary anthologies or classic Anaïs Nin (*Delta of Venus, Little Birds*). If films are more appealing but modern porn leaves you cold, try titillating foreign flicks like *Belle du Jour, Mediterraneo, Sirens, Sex and Lucia* (*Lucia y el Sexo*), and *Y Tu Mamá También*.

Never tried a sex toy? Or ready to try a new one? If you're feeling shy, skip the store visit and shop at your leisure at goodvibes.com, babeland.com, mypleasure.com, xandria.com, or comeasyouare.com. You'll keep that libido humming!

the good news is
Grooming? What's that?
Let yourself go for a while.

when in doubt, road trip

Thelma and Louise had it right: When life gets tough, the tough get in the car. Driving clears the head, reminds you that you're in the driver's seat, and shows you that there's life beyond your usual horizon. Pack up your vehicle with all the essentials: bottled water, Dr. Pepper, blanket, bikini, sunglasses, hiking boots, big funny hat, sunscreen, Doritos, camera, and, oh yeah, maps. Sing along to the radio or your favorite driving CDs, freeway flirt, stop at any picturesque barns or wineries or coastal trails that you run across, eat junk food, chat with the locals. (Remember how he was always trying to make good time?) You'll find that staring at that ribbon of highway is as good as any New Age meditation as far as opening your mind to possibility. Plus, on the road, you'll be reminded that change is always right around the bend. (Or at the very least, a Dairy Queen is!)

work a party, any party

Forgotten how to work a room? Well, accept all invites to parties or even a night out at your favorite watering hole and get your game on. If you overhear a friend or co-worker discussing a get-together, tell her how much fun that sounds. Use your recent breakup to your advantage and tell her you really need to get out of the house. Wear something saucy that shows off your best, um, ass-ets. Bring a small gift for the host (liquor is always appreciated). Kiss everyone you know and pick out a few cute boys you don't know to lipsmack on the cheek. Make sure your glass is always half full and if you find yourself talking to a bore, nicely excuse yourself to refresh your drink. Make a point to talk to at least five new people for at least five minutes each. Leave well before the party's over. They'll wonder if you were real or just a dream.

FEEL BETTER FAST: *Read a biography of an empowering woman, like Katharine Graham, Amelia Earhart, or Katharine Hepburn.*

self-sufficiency:
a primer

We all do it, especially when we're in a relationship.
We plead with our mate to perform relatively simple
"guy" tasks, because it's easier than figuring them out
ourselves. Banish this trend by setting aside one weekend day per month and dubbing it Self-Sufficiency
101. Learn to change a tire, buy stocks online, update
software, or fix a clogged pipe. Crack a beer when
you're done to celebrate.

kick it!

Feeling frustrated, cheated, confused, just plain angry? Take out your aggressions and get your body into dating shape simultaneously with this kickin' exercise. Craft a dummy out of pillows and your ex's old shirts, or tape his photo onto a punching bag. Then go to town! Kickboxing your ex to the curb is a much more satisfying way to get your endorphins flowing than running, sit-ups, or your 10,000th spinning class. Besides the sheer joy of pummeling his image, this exercise will give you a feeling of power and great glutes to boot. Take *that*!

pet therapy

After a breakup, it's perfectly normal to go through severe snuggle withdrawal. Get a dose of sweet, enthusiastic, unconditional love by offering to dog walk or pet sit for a friend or neighbor. A weekend of sleeping with a cuddly kitty or a run in the park with an adorable pooch might be just what the doctor ordered. (Plus, there's the added benefit of all the new hotties you'll encounter at the dog run.) If you've long been wanting to adopt a pet—perhaps holding off because your ex was unwilling or allergic—perhaps now's the time. If you're serious about it, go to your local animal shelter this weekend and bring home a frisky new playmate!

a weekend of wallowing

Sometimes, you just can't get up the energy to go out and mingle, even though you know you should. When that happens, go whole hog and dub it WOW (Weekend of Wallowing). Unplug the phone. Surround yourself with tissues and pillows. Wear your most comfortable sweats and listen to the most plaintive love songs you can dig up. Make an extensive list of all the things your ex will miss about you. Cry over old photos and letters. Get it out of your system, all in 48 hours! By Sunday night, you might be ready for a "misery loves company" movie marathon, where you can wallow in someone else's pain: cry along with *Terms of Endearment, Steel Magnolias,* or *Love Story.* By Monday morning, you'll be sick of sobbing and find yourself refreshed and ready to face the world.

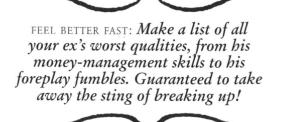

FEEL BETTER FAST: *Make a list of all your ex's worst qualities, from his money-management skills to his foreplay fumbles. Guaranteed to take away the sting of breaking up!*

draft a mission statement

What do you want, no, *require*, from your next relationship? Jot everything down in a personal mission statement. Declare what you will bring to the table and detail what you will embrace, accept, and refuse from the next guy to come knocking. Is it necessary that he rub your feet on a weekly basis? Want to have kids someday? Love teenage dramas on the WB? Bring you food when you're under the weather? Write it all down. Then, like Jerry Maguire, make 50 copies in the middle of the night and send it to all your girlfriends so they can hold you to your credo in the light of day.

practice the dark arts

LOVE POTION Concoct a love potion to leave 'em spellbound. In lieu of a cauldron, grab a small saucepan. Simmer ¼ cup of sweet almond oil or jojoba oil. Stirring in a clockwise motion, add a few drops each of these essential oils (or a combination of your choosing, depending on the qualities you want to coax the most): cinnamon (purifying), frankincense (calming), jasmine (sensual), lavender (relaxing), musk (sexy), orange blossom (invigorating), rose (intoxicating, calming), violet (passionate), and ylang ylang (aphrodisiac). Let cool. Pour into a glass container and store in a cool, dark place. Dab yourself liberally whenever you want to bewitch and bewilder.

VOODOO DOLL If you're feeling really crafty and a little bit witchy, make a "found object" voodoo doll out of crap He Who Shall Not Be Named left behind. Just stuff some of his rapidly shedding hair, metrosexual magazines, and other useless belongings in one of his old socks. Do with it what you will.

EX-ORCISM To perform an ex-orcism, recite a freedom chant as you burn something of his. You can make up your own chant or use our simple but effective poem to banish him forever:

I'm done with you,
I'm finally free,
God knows how much happier
I'm going to be.

Shimmy with gleeful release.

pin the tail on the ass

Celebrate a boyfriend-free birthday! Invite your single pals over and play party games from your youth, with a grown-up twist. Blow up a truly unflattering photo of your ex, tape it to a corkboard, and take turns pinning tails to it—go ahead, really stick that pin in. Or get a piñata in the shape of a donkey and pin his photo to the piñata's head; take turns bashing it until it pops open, revealing chocolates, condoms, and other treats. When it comes time to blow out the candles on your birthday cake, you'll know one wish has already come true—you've ditched the dead weight and are surrounded by people who love you. Happy birthday to you!

FEEL BETTER FAST: *Organize a girl's weekend at a spa, rented beach house, or fun hotel. Make it an annual event!*

single-girl skivvies

You know your underwear drawer: it contains the
undies he loved and the undies you love, and these
are not necessarily the same. It's time to purge! Besides
tossing aside any naughty bits that he gave you (you're
not possibly going to wear these on your upcoming
dates), take this opportunity to weed out anything
that just isn't your style and buy fresh and new.

embark on a rebound scavenger hunt

During your next girls' night out, mix things up by challenging your pals to a unique scavenger hunt. Only different kinds of men or items found on men will be gathered during this very cheeky contest. Here are a few suggested items to hunt down: a man born on foreign soil, a Leo, a condom from a bald man, a napkin or coaster with a man's sketch of you, a VP's business card . . . the possibilities are endless. Alternatively, you could bring along a Polaroid camera and dare your friends to do a bunch of outrageous things (with and to men, of course) in public. The most satisfying photos win!

FEEL BETTER FAST: *Hock the jewelry he gave you—or donate it—and buy yourself something fabulous.*

hot time in the city

Need a change of scenery? Look no farther than your own town. Get a weekend package at a swank hotel and invite several of your girlfriends to "get away" with you. Visit a sex shop, flirt with strangers in the hotel bar (make up fake identities for kicks—pretend to be flight attendants on layover, for instance), get some culture (pay attention to the naked male statues at your local museum), and order sundaes as you watch pay-per-view. Enjoy the hotel's spa, pool, or other amenities. Make sure to snap photos and buy souvenirs like tourists.

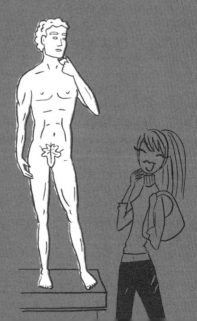

FEEL BETTER FAST: *Try one new thing in your town each month: the opera, ice hockey, book signings, or fringe theater.*

music therapy

Pull every empowering song you've belted out in the shower or the car and put it all on one tape or CD. Or burn a revenge CD to listen to when you're feeling particularly vindictive. While you're at it, get rid of all those CDs he left in your car or that remind you of him, and trade them at a used record store or sell them online. Swap out his Nickelback and Foreigner albums for some angry Ani DiFranco and Liz Phair.

EMPOWERED SINGLE GIRL SONG LIST
  "Goodbye Earl," Dixie Chicks
  "Goodbye to You," Scandal
  "There You Go," Pink
  "It's My Life," No Doubt
  "You Oughta Know," Alanis Morissette
  "Survivor," Destiny's Child
  "Shadowboxer," Fiona Apple
  "Toxic," Britney Spears
  "I'm Free," Violent Femmes
  Any number of songs by Pat Benatar

indulge your inner dominatrix

Turn negative energy into sexual energy by unleashing your inner vixen. When you want to rub him out (or at least give him a good flogging), think instead about tying up and pinning down a new cutie. Buy a new black bra or bustier, mesh stockings, and viciously high heels to get into character!

FEEL BETTER FAST: *Buy season tickets to something you don't normally go to. It will expand your horizons and your potential dating pool!*

it's a man hunt!

Don't limit yourself to bars or chat rooms—get creative to meet new men! You'll find plenty of sporty eligibles when you take your sweet-smelling self to batting cages, driving ranges, bowling alleys, or community softball games. Start keeping your eyes peeled at gas stations, libraries, and construction sites. Next time you hit the video store, car wash, or grocery aisles, take your time and sashay your way through your chores, keeping your antennae—and your chin—up. You'll see: Men are everywhere!

become the next sofia coppola

Shoot a film reenacting your breakup or your ideal fantasy relationship. It can be a comedy or tragedy— you choose! Use sock puppets, friends, stick figures, Play-Doh (easy to smash), whatever you want. For added verité, shoot with a jerky handheld camera and Super-8 film.

revenge fantasies

Daydream with a vengeance–think of the damage you could do to your ex! You could pin up a flyer with his name/photo in the men's room of his favorite bar ("Boy Toy loves pink cocktails, can recite from *Steel Magnolias,* and takes his footwear *very* seriously. Ask to see his Hummel collection!"); run a cringe-worthy personal ad on his behalf; or send embarrassing stuff (like gay cruise brochures or a subscription to *Cat Fancy*) to his office. Ahh, the possibilities are both endless and delicious . . . whether or not you would actually *do* these delectably devious things!

FEEL BETTER FAST: *This weekend, eat, drink, and say whatever you want without apologies to—or permission from—anyone.*

flirt with his friend(s)

Perhaps there were one or several pals or co-workers of your ex that made you think "if only..." Now's your chance! When you run into them, be flirty and happy. Or invite one of them out for a friendly drink and look drop-dead fabulous. Whether or not sparks fly with this guy, word *will* get back to your ex about how well you're doing (and looking).

shower yourself with jewels

Buy a terrific piece of jewelry and remind yourself that you don't need a man to have such things. Why not make it an annual ritual? Buy yourself one choice bauble on your birthday or Valentine's Day each year. Hunt for a piece that speaks to you. Maybe it's a ring by a female artist, maybe it's a pin with a meaningful phrase or stone that you spy at a craft fair. And maybe it's just Tiffany. Whatever it is, be sure to have it beautifully wrapped. After all, this is a gift. You're just giving it to yourself (and you know you won't have to return it!).

FEEL BETTER FAST: *Use his work e-mail address to sign him up for every spam-producing list you can think of, particularly unseemly ones.*

go *ahead, be petty*

You're allowed to be hurt, selfish, and downright petty right now. So do it up right! If he left his favorite cashmere sweater at your place, cut it up into cleaning rags. Better yet, fashion it into a smokin' skirt or tube top. If a special bottle of his wine was aging in your basement, drink it on a first date with someone else. Are his golf clubs still in your trunk? Donate them to Goodwill.

"stalk" a new guy

When you get the urge to drive by your ex's house or business, why not do a little recon and follow a new cutie instead? Google him, find an excuse to drop by his office, or take pains to be at the gym, café, or watering hole when you know he'll be there.

FEEL BETTER FAST: *Post warnings about him on dating Web sites.*

seduce yourself

Next Saturday night, take yourself out to dinner and a movie. Buy yourself a huge bouquet of flowers and a box of your favorite candy. Gaze at your bodacious bod in the mirror and tell yourself how freakin' hot you are. Narcissism isn't always such a bad thing.

pull a computer caper

If you know any of his passwords, hit your ex where it really hurts. While we don't condone making stock trades or wiring yourself cash from his online accounts (criminal charges could hinder your new social life), there are smaller, more personal ways to twist the knife via the keyboard. Trade the star player on his online fantasy baseball league for a couple of rookies. Send those endless spam chain letters he always hated to everyone in his address book.

a final word

Whether you've tried one ritual in this book or all fifty, rest assured that you're on the right track to soothing your trampled heart! And remember, extreme self-care doesn't end when you close this book. Indulge every craving, be patient with yourself, and rely on your friends for as long as you like. But most importantly, have as much fun as possible! Soon you'll be feeling better, stronger, and more fabulous than ever.

—Your friends, Kerry AND Jennifer

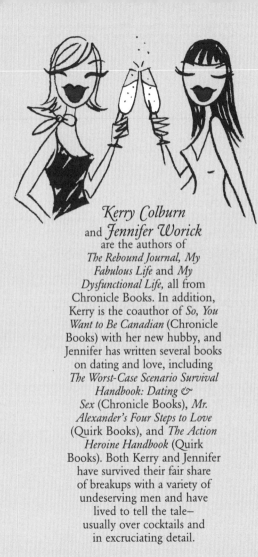

Kerry Colburn
and *Jennifer Worick*
are the authors of
*The Rebound Journal, My
Fabulous Life* and *My
Dysfunctional Life,* all from
Chronicle Books. In addition,
Kerry is the coauthor of *So, You
Want to Be Canadian* (Chronicle
Books) with her new hubby, and
Jennifer has written several books
on dating and love, including
*The Worst-Case Scenario Survival
Handbook: Dating &
Sex* (Chronicle Books), *Mr.
Alexander's Four Steps to Love*
(Quirk Books), and *The Action
Heroine Handbook* (Quirk
Books). Both Kerry and Jennifer
have survived their fair share
of breakups with a variety of
undeserving men and have
lived to tell the tale—
usually over cocktails and
in excruciating detail.